My Essential Planner

2021 My Essential Planner

Copyright © 2021 Malaika R. Kennie.

All rights reserved. No part of this book may be used or reproduced by any means, graphic, electronic, or mechanical, including photocopying, recording, taping or by any information storage retrieval system without the written permission of the author except in the case of brief quotations embodied in critical articles and reviews.

iUniverse books may be ordered through booksellers or by contacting:

iUniverse
1663 Liberty Drive
Bloomington, IN 47403
www.iuniverse.com
844-349-9409

Because of the dynamic nature of the Internet, any web addresses or links contained in this book may have changed since publication and may no longer be valid. The views expressed in this work are solely those of the author and do not necessarily reflect the views of the publisher, and the publisher hereby disclaims any responsibility for them.

Any people depicted in stock imagery provided by Getty Images are models, and such images are being used for illustrative purposes only.
Certain stock imagery © Getty Images.

ISBN: 978-1-6632-1495-9 (sc)
ISBN: 978-1-6632-1496-6 (e)

Print information available on the last page.

iUniverse rev. date: 12/21/2020

My Story

Trying to keep up with a busy household I was tired of managing my monthly budget in one book and my agenda planner and journal in another. I know I was not alone, so the birth of My Essential Planner was created. Instead of using separate books this 12 Month – Monthly/Weekly Budget, Agenda and Journal planner will make it easier to keep track of everything while staying inspirationally centered as you plan out your days, weeks and year.

Enjoy,
Malaika R. Kennie
MRK Collaboration Solutions

2021 At A Glance

JANUARY
MO	TU	WE	TH	FR	SA	SU
				1	2	3
4	5	6	7	8	9	10
11	12	13	14	15	16	17
18	19	20	21	22	23	24
25	26	27	28	29	30	31

FEBRUARY
MO	TU	WE	TH	FR	SA	SU
1	2	3	4	5	6	7
8	9	10	11	12	13	14
15	16	17	18	19	20	21
22	23	24	25	26	27	28

MARCH
MO	TU	WE	TH	FR	SA	SU
1	2	3	4	5	6	7
8	9	10	11	12	13	14
15	16	17	18	19	20	21
22	23	24	25	26	27	28
29	30	31				

APRIL
MO	TU	WE	TH	FR	SA	SU
			1	2	3	4
5	6	7	8	9	10	11
12	13	14	15	16	17	18
19	20	21	22	23	24	25
26	27	28	29	30		

MAY
MO	TU	WE	TH	FR	SA	SU
31					1	2
3	4	5	6	7	8	9
10	11	12	13	14	15	16
17	18	19	20	21	22	23
24	25	26	27	28	29	30

JUNE
MO	TU	WE	TH	FR	SA	SU
	1	2	3	4	5	6
7	8	9	10	11	12	13
14	15	16	17	18	19	20
21	22	23	24	25	26	27
28	29	30				

JULY
MO	TU	WE	TH	FR	SA	SU
			1	2	3	4
5	6	7	8	9	10	11
12	13	14	15	16	17	18
19	20	21	22	23	24	25
26	27	28	29	30	31	

AUGUST
MO	TU	WE	TH	FR	SA	SU
30	31					1
2	3	4	5	6	7	8
9	10	11	12	13	14	15
16	17	18	19	20	21	22
23	24	25	26	27	28	29

SEPTEMBER
MO	TU	WE	TH	FR	SA	SU
		1	2	3	4	5
6	7	8	9	10	11	12
13	14	15	16	17	18	19
20	21	22	23	24	25	26
27	28	29	30			

OCTOBER
MO	TU	WE	TH	FR	SA	SU
				1	2	3
4	5	6	7	8	9	10
11	12	13	14	15	16	17
18	19	20	21	22	23	24
25	26	27	28	29	30	31

NOVEMBER
MO	TU	WE	TH	FR	SA	SU
1	2	3	4	5	6	7
8	9	10	11	12	13	14
15	16	17	18	19	20	21
22	23	24	25	26	27	28
29	30					

DECEMBER
MO	TU	WE	TH	FR	SA	SU
		1	2	3	4	5
6	7	8	9	10	11	12
13	14	15	16	17	18	19
20	21	22	23	24	25	26
27	28	29	30	31		

2022 At A Glance

JANUARY

MO	TU	WE	TH	FR	SA	SU
31					1	2
3	4	5	6	7	8	9
10	11	12	13	14	15	16
17	18	19	20	21	22	23
24	25	26	27	28	29	30

FEBRUARY

MO	TU	WE	TH	FR	SA	SU
	1	2	3	4	5	6
7	8	9	10	11	12	13
14	15	16	17	18	19	20
21	22	23	24	25	26	27
28						

MARCH

MO	TU	WE	TH	FR	SA	SU
	1	2	3	4	5	6
7	8	9	10	11	12	13
14	15	16	17	18	19	20
21	22	23	24	25	26	27
28	29	30	31			

APRIL

MO	TU	WE	TH	FR	SA	SU
				1	2	3
4	5	6	7	8	9	10
11	12	13	14	15	16	17
18	19	20	21	22	23	24
25	26	27	28	29	30	

MAY

MO	TU	WE	TH	FR	SA	SU
30	31					1
2	3	4	5	6	7	8
9	10	11	12	13	14	15
16	17	18	19	20	21	22
23	24	25	26	27	28	29

JUNE

MO	TU	WE	TH	FR	SA	SU
		1	2	3	4	5
6	7	8	9	10	11	12
13	14	15	16	17	18	19
20	21	22	23	24	25	26
27	28	29	30			

JULY

MO	TU	WE	TH	FR	SA	SU
				1	2	3
4	5	6	7	8	9	10
11	12	13	14	15	16	17
18	19	20	21	22	23	24
25	26	27	28	29	30	31

AUGUST

MO	TU	WE	TH	FR	SA	SU
1	2	3	4	5	6	7
8	9	10	11	12	13	14
15	16	17	18	19	20	21
22	23	24	25	26	27	28
29	30	31				

SEPTEMBER

MO	TU	WE	TH	FR	SA	SU
			1	2	3	4
5	6	7	8	9	10	11
12	13	14	15	16	17	18
19	20	21	22	23	24	25
26	27	28	29	30		

OCTOBER

MO	TU	WE	TH	FR	SA	SU
31					1	2
3	4	5	6	7	8	9
10	11	12	13	14	15	16
17	18	19	20	21	22	23
24	25	26	27	28	29	30

NOVEMBER

MO	TU	WE	TH	FR	SA	SU
	1	2	3	4	5	6
7	8	9	10	11	12	13
14	15	16	17	18	19	20
21	22	23	24	25	26	27
28	29	30				

DECEMBER

MO	TU	WE	TH	FR	SA	SU
			1	2	3	4
5	6	7	8	9	10	11
12	13	14	15	16	17	18
19	20	21	22	23	24	25
26	27	28	29	30	31	

> "THE FIRST STEP TOWARDS GETTING SOMEWHERE IS TO DECIDE THAT YOU ARE NOT GOING TO STAY WHERE YOU ARE"
>
> — JOHN PIERPONT "JP" MORGAN

JAN

Monthly Budget

MONTH : YEAR :

INCOME

INCOME 1	INCOME 2	OTHER INCOME	TOTAL INCOME

BILLS TO BE PAID	DUE DATE	AMOUNT	PAID	NOTES
			○	
			○	
			○	
			○	
			○	
			○	
			○	
			○	
			○	
			○	
			○	
			○	
			○	
			○	

Notes

January

MONTHLY GOALS	MONDAY	TUESDAY	WEDNESDAY
	04	05	06
	11	12	13
IMPORTANT NOTES			
	18 *Martin Luther King Jr. Day*	19	20
	25	26	27

2021

THURSDAY	FRIDAY	SATURDAY	SUNDAY
	01 *New Years Day*	02	03
07	08	09	10
14	15	16	17
21	22	23	24
28	29	30	31

January Weekly View

28 MONDAY

29 TUESDAY

30 WEDNESDAY

2021

31 THURSDAY

01 FRIDAY

02 SATURDAY

03 SUNDAY

January Weekly View

04 MONDAY

05 TUESDAY

06 WEDNESDAY

2021

07 THURSDAY

08 FRIDAY

09 SATURDAY

10 SUNDAY

January Weekly View

11 MONDAY

12 TUESDAY

13 WEDNESDAY

2021

14 THURSDAY

15 FRIDAY

16 SATURDAY

17 SUNDAY

January Weekly View

18 MONDAY

19 TUESDAY

20 WEDNESDAY

2021

21 THURSDAY

22 FRIDAY

23 SATURDAY

24 SUNDAY

January Weekly View

25 MONDAY

26 TUESDAY

27 WEDNESDAY

2021

28 THURSDAY

29 FRIDAY

30 SATURDAY

31 SUNDAY

Notes

FEB

> "DO SOMETHING TODAY THAT YOUR FUTURE SELF WILL THANK YOU FOR"
>
> — SEAN PATRICK FLANERY

Monthly Budget

MONTH : YEAR :

INCOME

INCOME 1	INCOME 2	OTHER INCOME	TOTAL INCOME

BILLS TO BE PAID	DUE DATE	AMOUNT	PAID	NOTES
			○	
			○	
			○	
			○	
			○	
			○	
			○	
			○	
			○	
			○	
			○	
			○	
			○	
			○	
			○	

Notes

February

MONTHLY GOALS

IMPORTANT NOTES

MONDAY	TUESDAY	WEDNESDAY
01	02	03
08	09	10
15 *Presidents' Day*	16	17
22	23	24

2021

THURSDAY	FRIDAY	SATURDAY	SUNDAY
04	05	06	07
11	12	13	14 *Valentine's Day*
18	19	20	21
25	26	27	28

February Weekly View

01 MONDAY

02 TUESDAY

03 WEDNESDAY

2021

04 THURSDAY

05 FRIDAY

06 SATURDAY

07 SUNDAY

February Weekly View

08 MONDAY

09 TUESDAY

10 WEDNESDAY

2021

11 THURSDAY

12 FRIDAY

13 SATURDAY

14 SUNDAY

February Weekly View

15 MONDAY

16 TUESDAY

17 WEDNESDAY

2021

18 THURSDAY

19 FRIDAY

20 SATURDAY

21 SUNDAY

February Weekly View

22 MONDAY

23 TUESDAY

24 WEDNESDAY

2021

25 THURSDAY

26 FRIDAY

27 SATURDAY

28 SUNDAY

MAR

" AN INVESTMENT IN KNOWLEDGE ALWAYS PAYS THE BEST INTEREST

BENJAMIN FRANKLIN "

Monthly Budget

MONTH : YEAR :

INCOME

INCOME 1	INCOME 2	OTHER INCOME	TOTAL INCOME

BILLS TO BE PAID	DUE DATE	AMOUNT	PAID	NOTES
			○	
			○	
			○	
			○	
			○	
			○	
			○	
			○	
			○	
			○	
			○	
			○	
			○	
			○	

Notes

March

MONTHLY GOALS	MONDAY	TUESDAY	WEDNESDAY
	01	02	03
	08	09	10
	15	16	17
IMPORTANT NOTES	22	23	24
	29	30	31

2021

THURSDAY	FRIDAY	SATURDAY	SUNDAY
04	05	06	07
11	12	13	14
18	19	20	21
25	26	27	28

March Weekly View

01 MONDAY

02 TUESDAY

03 WEDNESDAY

2021

04 THURSDAY

05 FRIDAY

06 SATURDAY

07 SUNDAY

March Weekly View

08 MONDAY

09 TUESDAY

10 WEDNESDAY

2021

11 THURSDAY

12 FRIDAY

13 SATURDAY

14 SUNDAY

March Weekly View

15 MONDAY

16 TUESDAY

17 WEDNESDAY

2021

18 THURSDAY

19 FRIDAY

20 SATURDAY

21 SUNDAY

March Weekly View

22 MONDAY

23 TUESDAY

24 WEDNESDAY

2021

25 THURSDAY

26 FRIDAY

27 SATURDAY

28 SUNDAY

March Weekly View

29 MONDAY

30 TUESDAY

31 WEDNESDAY

2021

01 THURSDAY

02 FRIDAY

03 SATURDAY

04 SUNDAY

APR

> "SOMETIMES YOU HAVE TO CREATE YOUR OWN SUNSHINE"
>
> — SAM SUNDQUIST

Monthly Budget

MONTH : YEAR :

INCOME

INCOME 1	INCOME 2	OTHER INCOME	TOTAL INCOME

BILLS TO BE PAID	DUE DATE	AMOUNT	PAID	NOTES
			○	
			○	
			○	
			○	
			○	
			○	
			○	
			○	
			○	
			○	
			○	
			○	
			○	
			○	

April

MONTHLY GOALS

IMPORTANT NOTES

MONDAY	TUESDAY	WEDNESDAY
05	06	07
12	13	14
19	20	21
26	27	28

2021

THURSDAY	FRIDAY	SATURDAY	SUNDAY
01	02 *Good Friday*	03	04 *Easter Sunday*
08	09	10	11
15	16	17	18
22	23	24	25
29	30		

April Weekly View

05 MONDAY

06 TUESDAY

07 WEDNESDAY

2021

08 THURSDAY

09 FRIDAY

10 SATURDAY

11 SUNDAY

April Weekly View

12 MONDAY

13 TUESDAY

14 WEDNESDAY

2021

15 THURSDAY

16 FRIDAY

17 SATURDAY

18 SUNDAY

April Weekly View

19 MONDAY

20 TUESDAY

21 WEDNESDAY

2021

22 THURSDAY

23 FRIDAY

24 SATURDAY

25 SUNDAY

April Weekly View

26 MONDAY

27 TUESDAY

28 WEDNESDAY

2021

29 THURSDAY

30 FRIDAY

01 SATURDAY

02 SUNDAY

MAY

> "DON'T COMPARE YOURSELF TO OTHERS. BE LIKE THE SUN AND THE MOON AND SHINE WHEN IT'S YOUR TIME"
>
> — UNKNOWN

Monthly Budget

MONTH : YEAR :

INCOME

INCOME 1	INCOME 2	OTHER INCOME	TOTAL INCOME

BILLS TO BE PAID	DUE DATE	AMOUNT	PAID	NOTES
			○	
			○	
			○	
			○	
			○	
			○	
			○	
			○	
			○	
			○	
			○	
			○	
			○	
			○	
			○	

Notes

May

MONTHLY GOALS

IMPORTANT NOTES

MONDAY	TUESDAY	WEDNESDAY
03	04	05
10	11	12
17	18	19
24	25	26
31 *Memorial Day*		

2021

THURSDAY	FRIDAY	SATURDAY	SUNDAY
		01	02
06	07	08	09 *Mother's Day*
13	14	15	16
20	21	22	23
27	28	29	30

May Weekly View

03 MONDAY

04 TUESDAY

05 WEDNESDAY

2021

06 THURSDAY

07 FRIDAY

08 SATURDAY

09 SUNDAY

May Weekly View

10 MONDAY

11 TUESDAY

12 WEDNESDAY

2021

13 THURSDAY

14 FRIDAY

15 SATURDAY

16 SUNDAY

May Weekly View

17 MONDAY

18 TUESDAY

19 WEDNESDAY

2021

20 THURSDAY

21 FRIDAY

22 SATURDAY

23 SUNDAY

May Weekly View

24 MONDAY

25 TUESDAY

26 WEDNESDAY

2021

27 THURSDAY

28 FRIDAY

29 SATURDAY

30 SUNDAY

May Weekly View

31 MONDAY

01 TUESDAY

03 WEDNESDAY

2021

03 THURSDAY

04 FRIDAY

05 SATURDAY

06 SUNDAY

Notes

JUN

> "WHEN YOU FEEL LIKE GIVING UP JUST REMEMBER THAT THERE IS A LOT OF PEOPLE YOU STILL HAVE TO PROVE WRONG."
>
> UNKNOWN

Monthly Budget

MONTH : YEAR :

INCOME

INCOME 1	INCOME 2	OTHER INCOME	TOTAL INCOME

BILLS TO BE PAID	DUE DATE	AMOUNT	PAID	NOTES
			○	
			○	
			○	
			○	
			○	
			○	
			○	
			○	
			○	
			○	
			○	
			○	
			○	
			○	
			○	

Notes

June

MONTHLY GOALS	MONDAY	TUESDAY	WEDNESDAY
		01	02
	07	08	09
	14	15	16
IMPORTANT NOTES	21	22	23
	28	29	30

2021

THURSDAY	FRIDAY	SATURDAY	SUNDAY
03	04 *National Donut Day*	05	06
10	11	12	13
17	18	19	20 *Father's Day*
24	25	26	27

June Weekly View

07 MONDAY

08 TUESDAY

09 WEDNESDAY

2021

10 THURSDAY

11 FRIDAY

12 SATURDAY

13 SUNDAY

June Weekly View

14 MONDAY

15 TUESDAY

16 WEDNESDAY

2021

17 THURSDAY

18 FRIDAY

19 SATURDAY

20 SUNDAY

June Weekly View

21 MONDAY

22 TUESDAY

23 WEDNESDAY

2021

24 THURSDAY

25 FRIDAY

26 SATURDAY

27 SUNDAY

June Weekly View

28 MONDAY

29 TUESDAY

30 WEDNESDAY

2021

01 THURSDAY

02 FRIDAY

03 SATURDAY

04 SUNDAY

> "Our greatest glory is not in never falling, but in raising every time we fall"
>
> — CONFUCIUS

Monthly Budget

MONTH: YEAR:

INCOME

INCOME 1	INCOME 2	OTHER INCOME	TOTAL INCOME

BILLS TO BE PAID	DUE DATE	AMOUNT	PAID	NOTES
			○	
			○	
			○	
			○	
			○	
			○	
			○	
			○	
			○	
			○	
			○	
			○	
			○	
			○	
			○	

Notes

July

MONTHLY GOALS

MONDAY	TUESDAY	WEDNESDAY
05 *Independence Day Holiday*	06	07
12	13	14
19	20	21
26	27	28

IMPORTANT NOTES

2021

THURSDAY	FRIDAY	SATURDAY	SUNDAY
01	02	03	04 *Independence Day*
08	09	10	11
15	16	17	18
22	23	24	25
29	30	31	

July Weekly View

05 MONDAY

06 TUESDAY

07 WEDNESDAY

2021

08 THURSDAY

09 FRIDAY

10 SATURDAY

11 SUNDAY

July Weekly View

12 MONDAY

13 TUESDAY

14 WEDNESDAY

2021

14 THURSDAY

16 FRIDAY

17 SATURDAY

18 SUNDAY

July Weekly View

19 MONDAY

20 TUESDAY

21 WEDNESDAY

2021

22 THURSDAY

23 FRIDAY

24 SATURDAY

25 SUNDAY

July Weekly View

26 MONDAY

27 TUESDAY

28 WEDNESDAY

2021

29 THURSDAY

30 FRIDAY

31 SATURDAY

01 SUNDAY

Notes

AUG

> "IF YOUR DREAMS DON'T SCARE YOU, THEY ARE TOO SMALL
>
> RICHARD BRANSON"

Monthly Budget

MONTH : YEAR :

INCOME

INCOME 1	INCOME 2	OTHER INCOME	TOTAL INCOME

BILLS TO BE PAID	DUE DATE	AMOUNT	PAID	NOTES
			○	
			○	
			○	
			○	
			○	
			○	
			○	
			○	
			○	
			○	
			○	
			○	
			○	
			○	
			○	

August

MONTHLY GOALS

IMPORTANT NOTES

MONDAY	TUESDAY	WEDNESDAY
02	03	04
09	10	11
16	17	18
23	24	25
30	31	

THURSDAY	FRIDAY	SATURDAY	SUNDAY
			01
05	06	07	08
12	13	14	15
19	20	21	22
26	27	28	29

2021

August Weekly View

02 MONDAY

03 TUESDAY

04 WEDNESDAY

2021

05 THURSDAY

06 FRIDAY

07 SATURDAY

08 SUNDAY

09 MONDAY

10 TUESDAY

11 WEDNESDAY

2021

12 THURSDAY

13 FRIDAY

14 SATURDAY

15 SUNDAY

August Weekly View

16 MONDAY

17 TUESDAY

18 WEDNESDAY

2021

19 THURSDAY

20 FRIDAY

21 SATURDAY

22 SUNDAY

August Weekly View

23 MONDAY

24 TUESDAY

25 WEDNESDAY

2021

26 THURSDAY

27 FRIDAY

28 SATURDAY

29 SUNDAY

August Weekly View

30 MONDAY

31 TUESDAY

01 WEDNESDAY

2021

02 THURSDAY

03 FRIDAY

04 SATURDAY

05 SUNDAY

> "IF YOU DON'T LIKE SOMETHING, CHANGE IT. IF YOU CAN'T CHANGE IT, CHANGE YOUR ATTITUDE"
>
> MAYA ANGELOU

SEP

Monthly Budget

MONTH : YEAR :

INCOME

INCOME 1	INCOME 2	OTHER INCOME	TOTAL INCOME

BILLS TO BE PAID	DUE DATE	AMOUNT	PAID	NOTES
			○	
			○	
			○	
			○	
			○	
			○	
			○	
			○	
			○	
			○	
			○	
			○	
			○	
			○	
			○	

Notes

September

MONTHLY GOALS

IMPORTANT NOTES

MONDAY	TUESDAY	WEDNESDAY
		01
06 *Labor Day*	07	08
13	14	15
20	21	22
27	28	29

2021

THURSDAY	FRIDAY	SATURDAY	SUNDAY
02	03	04	05
09	10	11	12
16	17	18	19
23	24	25	26
30			

September Weekly View

06 MONDAY

07 TUESDAY

08 WEDNESDAY

2021

09 THURSDAY

10 FRIDAY

11 SATURDAY

12 SUNDAY

September Weekly View

13 MONDAY

14 TUESDAY

15 WEDNESDAY

2021

16 THURSDAY

17 FRIDAY

18 SATURDAY

19 SUNDAY

September Weekly View

20 MONDAY

21 TUESDAY

22 WEDNESDAY

2021

23 THURSDAY

24 FRIDAY

25 SATURDAY

26 SUNDAY

September Weekly View

27 MONDAY

28 TUESDAY

29 WEDNESDAY

2021

30 THURSDAY

01 FRIDAY

02 SATURDAY

03 SUNDAY

OCT

> "NEVER GIVE UP. GREAT THINGS TAKE TIME"
>
> — DHIREN PRAJAPATI

Monthly Budget

MONTH: YEAR:

INCOME

INCOME 1	INCOME 2	OTHER INCOME	TOTAL INCOME

BILLS TO BE PAID	DUE DATE	AMOUNT	PAID	NOTES
			○	
			○	
			○	
			○	
			○	
			○	
			○	
			○	
			○	
			○	
			○	
			○	
			○	
			○	
			○	

October

MONTHLY GOALS

IMPORTANT NOTES

MONDAY	TUESDAY	WEDNESDAY
04	05	06
11 *Columbus Day*	12	13
18	19	20
25	26	27

2021

THURSDAY	FRIDAY	SATURDAY	SUNDAY
	01	02	03
07	08	09	10
14	15	16	17
21	22	23	24
28	29	30	31 *Halloween*

October Weekly View

04 MONDAY

05 TUESDAY

06 WEDNESDAY

2021

07 THURSDAY

08 FRIDAY

09 SATURDAY

10 SUNDAY

October Weekly View

11 MONDAY

12 TUESDAY

13 WEDNESDAY

2021

14 THURSDAY

15 FRIDAY

16 SATURDAY

17 SUNDAY

October Weekly View

18 MONDAY

19 TUESDAY

20 WEDNESDAY

2021

21 THURSDAY

22 FRIDAY

23 SATURDAY

24 SUNDAY

October Weekly View

25 MONDAY

26 TUESDAY

27 WEDNESDAY

2021

28 THURSDAY

29 FRIDAY

30 SATURDAY

31 SUNDAY

> **LEARN TO BE THANKFUL FOR WHAT YOU ALREADY HAVE WHILE YOU PURSUE ALL THAT YOU WANT**
>
> — JIM ROHN

NOV

Monthly Budget

MONTH : YEAR :

INCOME

INCOME 1	INCOME 2	OTHER INCOME	TOTAL INCOME

BILLS TO BE PAID	DUE DATE	AMOUNT	PAID	NOTES
			○	
			○	
			○	
			○	
			○	
			○	
			○	
			○	
			○	
			○	
			○	
			○	
			○	
			○	

Notes

November

MONTHLY GOALS	MONDAY	TUESDAY	WEDNESDAY
	01	02	03
	08	09	10
	15	16	17
IMPORTANT NOTES	22	23	24
	29	30	

2021

THURSDAY	FRIDAY	SATURDAY	SUNDAY
04	05	06	07
11 *Veterans Day*	12	13	14
18	19	20	21
25 *Thanksgiving Day*	26	27	28

November Weekly View

08 MONDAY

09 TUESDAY

10 WEDNESDAY

2021

11 THURSDAY

12 FRIDAY

13 SATURDAY

14 SUNDAY

November Weekly View

15 MONDAY

16 TUESDAY

17 WEDNESDAY

2021

18 THURSDAY

19 FRIDAY

20 SATURDAY

21 SUNDAY

November Weekly View

22 MONDAY

23 TUESDAY

24 WEDNESDAY

2021

25 THURSDAY

26 FRIDAY

27 SATURDAY

28 SUNDAY

November Weekly View

29 MONDAY

30 TUESDAY

01 WEDNESDAY

2021

02 THURSDAY

03 FRIDAY

04 SATURDAY

05 SUNDAY

Notes

DEC

> "TODAY IS YOUR OPPORTUNITY TO BUILD THE TOMORROW YOU WANT"
>
> — KEN POIROT

Monthly Budget

MONTH : YEAR :

INCOME

INCOME 1	INCOME 2	OTHER INCOME	TOTAL INCOME

BILLS TO BE PAID	DUE DATE	AMOUNT	PAID	NOTES
			○	
			○	
			○	
			○	
			○	
			○	
			○	
			○	
			○	
			○	
			○	
			○	
			○	
			○	
			○	

Notes

December

MONTHLY GOALS	MONDAY	TUESDAY	WEDNESDAY
			01
	06	07	08
	13	14	15
IMPORTANT NOTES	20	21	22
	27	28	29

2021

THURSDAY	FRIDAY	SATURDAY	SUNDAY
02	03	04	05
09	10	11	12
16	17	18	19
23	24	25 *Christmas*	26
30	31		

December Weekly View

06 MONDAY

07 TUESDAY

08 WEDNESDAY

2021

09 THURSDAY

10 FRIDAY

11 SATURDAY

12 SUNDAY

December Weekly View

13 MONDAY

14 TUESDAY

15 WEDNESDAY

2021

16 THURSDAY

17 FRIDAY

18 SATURDAY

19 SUNDAY

December Weekly View

20 MONDAY

21 TUESDAY

22 WEDNESDAY

2021

23 THURSDAY

24 FRIDAY

25 SATURDAY

26 SUNDAY

December Weekly View

27 MONDAY

28 TUESDAY

29 WEDNESDAY

2021

30 THURSDAY

31 FRIDAY

01 SATURDAY

02 SUNDAY

Notes

CPSIA information can be obtained
at www.ICGtesting.com
Printed in the USA
BVHW022313050121
597069BV00006B/28